'MURDER'

AND THE

MONARCHY

of seven English kings
together with a further four
who died in battle

by

Reverend A. Tindal Hart

William Sessions Limited
The Ebor Press
York, England

ISBN 1 85072 027 4

Printed in 11/12 point Plantin Typeface
by William Sessions Limited
The Ebor Press, York, England

Contents

I Definitely or Possibly Murdered

II Monarchs Killed in Battle

Illustrations

Preface

FOR THOUSANDS OF YEARS kingship in its various forms, representing the leadership of one man both in war and peace, and normally on an hereditary basis, was accepted by most people in the world as the natural form of government for their respective communities. Its status was usually enhanced not only by a stately and elaborate ceremonial, but often also by a religious aura. The kings of Israel and Judah for example claimed to be 'The Lord's Anointed'; and one could quote the God-Emperors of Rome, the German Holy Roman Emperors; and in 17th century England, the doctrines of 'The Divine Right of Kings' and 'The King can do no Wrong'. Yet even in its hey-day monarchy always remained constantly under threat from violent death: either by overthrow in war, successful revolution, or assassination. 'Uneasy lies the head that wears a crown' wrote Shakespeare, and this has never been more amply illustrated than in the Kingdom of England, where from the Conquest to the present time, seven of our monarchs may have been murdered. Yet curiously enough each of them suffered a different method of execution, ranging from shooting, poison and starvation, to the more dramatic deaths of having a red-hot iron inserted into the bowels, by clubbing, smothering and beheading. Three of the victims were later designated as martyrs, and one only narrowly failed to attain canonisation. The majority probably did not deserve to die, but in two cases at least I think England was well rid of them.

The College of St. Barnabas,
Lingfield, Surrey,   A. Tindal Hart

Murder and the Monarchy

I Definitely or Possibly Murdered

William II (1087-1100): William Rufus, the Red King, so-called from his ruddy countenance, was probably one of the most ruthless, hated and godless of all our English monarchs. Yet he was also one of the most able and efficient. On the death of his father, William the Conqueror, he secured the throne, which was rightfully the inheritance of his eldest brother, Robert; and then, when the latter was away on a crusade, also took possession of his brother's patrimony of Normandy. Rufus openly scoffed both in public and private at religion, and savagely persecuted the Church. Curiously, however, he was never excommunicated by the Pope, nor was England put under an interdict, thanks to the intercession of Anselm, then Archbishop of Canterbury.

Rufus was a ruthless tyrant who ruled the country with a rod of iron, and was generally hated by high and low alike. The full story of Rufus has not yet been written in the history books, and here we are simply concerned with his death. In the summer of 1100 he was preparing a great fleet, and assembling a large army for the invasion of France: 'in order', wrote the English Chronicler, 'to win for himself the mastery of all Western Gaul from the Channel to the Garonne'.

However, on 1 August, Rufus was riding with a party at Brockenhurst, intending to enjoy his favourite sport of hunting in the New Forest the next day. Here one of his companions asked: 'Where will you keep next Christmas?', to which the king replied, 'Poitiers'.

On 2 August 1100 they went hunting, during which Rufus was shot and killed by an arrow. He was only 43 years old and unmarried and it has never been clearly established whether his death was accident or murder; or, indeed, who actually shot him. All the English Chronicler has recorded about this fatal event runs as follows: 'Thereafter on the morrow [2 August] was King William shot off with an arrow from his own men in hunting'. Yet is it not strange that his 'own men' then apparently fled for their lives, leaving neighbouring peasants to find the body, wrap it in a cloth, lay it upon a cart, and bring it to Winchester, where it was buried immediately in the cathedral under the central tower, 'out of reverence for the royal dignity'. However, there were no religious services either during or after the interment; and the clergy of Winchester, backed by the laity, flatly refused to allow any masses to be said or bells tolled for his soul, whose life and reign, they felt, had put him beyond the pale of christian fellowship.

'Though I hesitate to say it', wrote the English Chronicler, 'all things that are loathsome to God and to earnest men were customary in this land at that time, and therefore he was loathsome to nigh all his people, and abominable to God, as his end showed, forasmuch that he departed in the midst of his unrighteousness, without repentance and expiation'. Seven years later the tower, under which he lay, collapsed, and this it was believed revealed God's judgment that Rufus was not fit for burial in consecrated ground. Rufus' grave now lies in the Lady Chapel at Winchester, covered by a black marble slab, but containing no inscription.

Was Rufus murdered? The answer apparently is in the affirmative. William Tirel, who is generally supposed to have fired the arrow, immediately rode post-haste to the nearest port and sailed for France, where he was the Lord of Poix in Ponthieu. From this safe haven he strongly denied under oath that he had killed the king, declaring that he was not even in Rufus' company at the time, and had not seen him all day. But Tirel's two brothers-in-law, Gilbert and Roger Clare, were certainly members of the small hunting party surrounding the king; and so was Rufus' youngest brother, Henry.

It is perhaps significant that Henry, totally disregarding the dead king, rode straight to Winchester in order to seize the royal treasury and have himself elected to the throne. Three days later, on 5 August 1100, he was crowned Henry I at Westminster. Then, when he was firmly in control, he treated the Clare family with marked favour. The evidence therefore points to the fact that the sudden end of Rufus was the result of a conspiracy, formed and organised by the House of Clare, of which Henry I himself was well aware.

King John (1199-1216), another cruel and ruthless monarch, who had the unpleasant habit of torturing and starving his prisoners to death, lacked both Rufus' efficiency and courage. An incompetent blunderer, he was primarily responsible for his own disastrous reign. He offended the baronage by his divorce of Isabella of Gloucester, whose gallants he hanged over her bed, whilst imprisoning the queen herself at Gloucester. His second marriage to Isabella of Anglouleme, the betrothed of Hugh of Lusignan, lost him Poitou; and the murder of his nephew Arthur, at Rouen, lost him Normandy. The free rein he gave to his mercenary army for indiscriminate plunder, rape and murder, alienated the country as a whole.

By refusing to accept Stephen Langton, the nominee of Pope Innocent III, as Archbishop of Canterbury, he brought down upon England a papal interdict, which was only lifted when John abjectly agreed to accept the country back by becoming a papal fief: an action that mortally offended England's pride. The final straw was his rash invasion of France in 1214, leading to the disastrous defeat of Bouvines, the loss of all his available resources, and further demands for military service and scrutages from the feudal classes, which decided the barons to break his tyrannical rule once and for ever.

They banded together and compelled John to sign with his mark the Magna Carta at Runnymede in June 1215. False as ever, the king quickly broke his promises, and the result was civil war. At first John was successful, subduing the north and east, and largely confining the rebel power to London. But on 27 February 1216 the French arrived in the person of the Dauphin, Louis, and the tables were quickly turned. Hugh de Burgh held out in Dover, but Louis, having received the homage of the barons as their next king, succeeded in overrunning most of the south and east of the country;

whilst the Scots invaded the north. John moved to intercept the latter, doing as much damage as possible on the way. 'Everywhere', wrote the Chronicler, 'he ravaged mercilessly, even destroying the churches.' He succeeded in raising the seige of Lincoln, pillaged Crowland Abbey, and then turned south to defeat a contingent of the rebels at King's Lynn.

At this time he was in good health, riding fifty miles a day, and yet able to attend to business before he slept. Deciding to return to Lincolnshire, John and his army moved round the Wash along a circuitous road by Wisbech; but sent his baggage, including his treasure, which then contained one of the finest collections of jewellery in Europe, by a shorter route, only passable at low tide, across the four and a half mile estuary of the Wellstream River, now known as the Nene, between Cross Keys and Long Sutton, led by local guides. This journey was never completed. The whole convoy of men, horses, treasure, wardrobe, moveable chapel and relics, was either swept away by the incoming tide or swallowed up in quicksands. No-one survived to tell the tale, and nothing was ever recovered.

On the evening of that disaster, 12 October 1216, John himself reached the Cistercian Abbey of Swineshead, where he is said to have indulged unwisely in an orgy of eating and drinking. Two days later, a very sick man, he reached Sleaford and was bled by his physician, the Abbot of Croxton. With great difficulty he struggled on to Newark, and here the abbot heard his confession and gave him the sacrament. He made a short and dignified Will, in which he nominated his nine-year-old son, Henry (III), as his successor; and died on 19 October at the age of 50.

In accordance with his directions he was buried in the cathedral church of Worcester in front of the High Altar, between the two saints Wulfstan and Oswald. There was at that time a well-known medieval device whereby a notorious sinner would don a monk's habit and cowl on his death-bed, hoping thereby to creep into heaven thus disguised. It was known as *Ad Succurendum*. When John's tomb was opened in 1797 he was found to be wearing a monk's cowl. No doubt he also hoped that the two saints on either side of him would intercede on his behalf at the Last Judgment; but alas, their tombs were destroyed at the Reformation and their bones scattered. (It is possible, however, that they were re-interred in the present Sanctuary.) So now King John lies there in solitary state, and must fend for himself.

But was he murdered? It seems very likely. There are two stories extant: the first is that his beer was poisoned by a Swineshead monk, because the king, in his cups, had threatened to violate the abbot's sister, a nun; but the second and more probable tale is that the same monk or another served John with poisoned pears, after hearing him boasting that his mercenaries would destroy all the harvests in the neighbourhood, thus creating a famine and so compelling his enemies to submit. A vegetable poison of this kind might well have produced the symptoms from which he suffered, namely dysentry and vomiting, leading on to the fever that killed him. As soon as it was known that John was dead, the country as a whole quickly rallied to the side of his son, Henry III; and the French, defeated both by land and sea, were expelled.

King Edward II (1307-1327) was a fine physical specimen like his father Edward I; but appeared destitute of any serious purpose, being the first king after the Conquest to be uninterested in business, devoting himself instead to athletic games and playing with mechanical toys, whilst allowing his favourites to dictate his actions. He had married Isabella, the daughter of Charles the Fair of France, the so-called 'she-wolf of France'; and by her had two sons and several daughters. Yet, like William Rufus before him, he was primarily an homosexual, and contracted intimate relationships with two young men, Piers Gaveston and Hugh le Despenser the younger. The scandalised barons, led by Thomas of Lancaster, rebelled and put Gaveston to death. Edward replied by allying himself with the powerful Hugh le Despenser the elder, the father of his new favourite; whereupon in 1321 the barons succeeded in persuading parliament to exile both of them.

This action for once stirred Edward into a vigorous response. He raised an army, crushed the Welsh Lords and Thomas of Lancaster at the Battle of Boroughbridge in 1322, and had Thomas hanged at Pontefract. However, on the intercession of Queen Isabella, he

King John's Tomb in Worcester Cathedral

Tomb of King Edward II in Gloucester Cathedral

commuted the death sentence of Roger Mortimer, the most powerful of the Welsh Lords, to perpetual imprisonment in the Tower of London.

For the next five years the Despensers ruled England, heaping up wealth for themselves and causing considerable popular discontent. Then in disgust at what was happening Isabella went over to France, ostensibly to negotiate with her brother the return of Gascony, which he had seized; whilst Roger, escaping from the Tower, joined her, and they became lovers. She now persuaded her husband to allow their eldest son, the future Edward III, to go to France in order to do homage for Gascony; and, using him as the legitimate heir, together with Roger and a band of other exiles, landed at Orwell in Suffolk during September 1326. At first their only demands were for the destruction of the Despensers and revenge for Thomas; but, when they found the country as a whole rallying to their side, they decided to aim for the kingdom.

Deserted by the Londoners and unable to raise an army, Edward fled westwards to the estates of the Despensers in Gloucestershire. The elder Despenser went to Bristol, where he was arrested and executed; whilst the king, failing to find help anywhere, took boat to Lundy Island, only to be driven back by a storm. He, together with his chancellor, Baldock, and the younger Despenser were captured by Henry of Lancaster at Neath, when the last two were handed over to the queen at Hereford and hanged. Edward himself was taken to Kenilworth Castle, where he was kindly treated by his cousin.

Meanwhile parliament had met, and on 7 January 1327 deposed the king, electing his son as their next monarch. But the 15-year-old Edward (III) refused to accept the crown without his father's consent; so a committee of bishops and barons went to Kenilworth to demand the latter's resignation. Edward listened to them in tears, lamenting his fate and evil counsellors, but rejoicing that his son would succeed him. He remained at Kenilworth until the spring, comfortably housed and honourably treated, yet complaining of his separation from wife and family. This state of affairs could not continue. Isabella and Mortimer were well aware of their own precarious hold on power, and dared not leave Edward alive. Already one plot to rescue him had been uncovered; so the question remained how was he to die? By natural means if possible. The two knights Thomas de Gournay and John Maltravers were sent to remove him from Kenilworth and cart him about up and down the country, treating the ex-king as cruelly as possible during these wanderings. For example he was given very little food, insufficient clothing, crowned with evil-smelling hay and shaved by the roadside with ditchwater.

Eventually they arrived at Berkeley Castle in Gloucestershire, whose owner was removed, and Edward placed in a pestilence-ridden chamber over a charnel house. Still his robust Plantagenet constitution continued to resist all such methods to kill him, for he was but 43 years old. Two attempts were now made to rescue him. The first, led by a Dominican friar, Thomas Dunhead, actually succeeded for a time, the king being freed from his dungeon and transported to Corfe Castle, where, however, he was recaptured. Dunhead died a horrible death. The second conspiracy, organised in Wales by Sir Rhys ap Griffith, was discovered in time and nipped in the bud. Isabella and Roger now decided that a more drastic solution was needed, and the two jailers were advised accordingly. So, on the evening of 27 September 1327, the king was taken to a comfortable apartment, assured that his privations were over, given a lavish meal with a great deal of alcohol, and then undressed and put into a soft bed. Immediately he fell into a deep alcohol-induced sleep. In the middle of the night his murderers rushed in, removed the coverlets, and whilst one of them held him down, another thrust a red-hot iron through the anus into the bowels. The shrieks of the dying king reverberated throughout the castle and could even be heard in the street outside. None the less it was given out that he had died naturally, and his body was exposed to the public, showing no obvious outward signs of violence.

Edward II was then buried with considerable pomp in Gloucester Abbey church, later the cathedral, where his son eventually caused a magnificent tomb to be erected over his grave. Quickly forgetting his many sins and weaknesses, and more than half suspecting murder, he soon became in the eyes of the populace a saint and a martyr. Miracles, or so it was said, were wrought at his shrine, which right up to the Reformation attracted a continuous flow of pilgrims. For their accommodation the famous New Inn was built nearby.

Isabella and Mortimer did not, as they had hoped, benefit from this murder. Indeed, rumours continued to spread that Edward II was still alive; and in 1328 there was yet another formidable conspiracy in his favour, led by the Earl of Kent. Furthermore it was long believed in certain quarters that the ex-king had escaped abroad and ended his days as a hermit in Lombardy. Isabella shed hypocritical tears for her husband at the coronation of Edward III; but they did not influence the new king, who, once he had consolidated his position, and disgusted at the way his mother was living openly with Mortimer, decided to act. With a band of friends he entered Nottingham Castle, where the lovers were staying, through a secret passage, and surprised the couple in each others' arms. Mortimer was seized, despite the queen's frantic cry: 'Fair son, have mercy on the gentle Mortimer'. The latter was condemned to death without a trial for the murder of the late king, together with his abettor, Sir Simon Bereford, and they were both hanged, drawn and quartered at Tyburn, the first criminals to be executed there.

Drawing a discreet veil over his mother's involvement in the murder, Edward III had her honourably confined at Castle Rising in Norfolk, where he used to visit her from time to time. She was not openly kept in custody, but would play no further part in public affairs. She died in 1358, and was interred with Mortimer in Grey Friars Church, London, where, 'carrying her hypocrisy even to the grave, she was buried with the heart of her husband on her breast'. Her statuette is one of 'the weepers' on the tomb of her second son, John of Eltham, and her head is also on a carving in Winchelsea Church.

What happened to the actual murderers? Judicial proceedings were taken against de Gournay and Maltravers, together with another accomplice, Ogle. The first and last were found guilty of murder, and Maltravers of being an accessory; but all three escaped punishment by flight abroad. De Gournay and Ogle died in exile, whilst Maltravers eventually had his sentence of outlawry remitted. His estates were restored, he became a Member of Parliament, and died in his bed at a ripe old age in 1361.

King Richard II (1377-1399). His last three years of autocratic rule alienated most of the country and whilst Richard was in Ireland with his army, Henry Bolingbroke landed at Ravenspur in Yorkshire during July 1399. Ostensibly he had simply returned to claim his forfeited Dukedom of Lancaster; but, when he found the strongest elements in England rallying to his side, he decided instead, during a triumphant march south, to make a Lancastrian bid for the throne. Richard, hearing of the invasion, hastened home; but the men he brought with him either deserted or had to be disbanded at Milford Haven, before the king himself fled north to Conway Castle, where he was met by the Earl of Northumberland and Archbishop Arundel of Canterbury, negotiating on Henry's behalf.

The story that Richard told them that he was willing to abdicate the throne is a Lancastrian fable. Instead he was deluded into believing that once he had allowed his evil counsellors to be dealt with, he could retain the kingship. Deceived by these promises he was lured to Flint, arrested, and taken first to Chester and then brought south to London. Here he was lodged in the Tower, and the strongest pressure was brought to bear upon him to sign an abdication deed. This he eventually did, handing over his signet ring to Henry (IV); but in a gesture characteristic of the man he threw his crown on the ground, saying he surrendered it to God and not to Bolingbroke.

This abdication document, together with the signet ring, were put before an hastily assembled parliament that promptly approved Richard's renunciation of the crown, electing Henry as his successor. At the same time a long list of grievances against the late king was read, and the demand made that he should be brought to trial. This was refused, and so Richard was never given any opportunity of defending himself. Instead the House of Lords condemned him to perpetual imprisonment, 'to be', ran the decree, 'removed to a safe custody where no mob could rescue him and no former member of his household should have access to him'.

Consequently, shortly after Henry IV's coronation on 25 October 1399, Richard was moved in disguise from the Tower to Gravesend and from there to Leeds Castle in Kent. Finally he was transferred to Pontefract Castle in Yorkshire and put into the custody of Robert

Waterman and Sir Thomas Swinford. But early in the New Year 1400 there was a rebellion in his favour, led by the disgruntled Earls of Kent, Rutland, Huntingdon and Salisbury, all of whom had been deprived of their dukedoms by the new king. The rumour was spread that Richard himself had escaped, and for a time he was impersonated by a priest named Maudelyn. The plan was to seize Henry, then staying at Windsor; but it misfired, for the new king got wind of the plot in time, and fled to London, which rallied to his support. Then, after an indecisive skirmish, the rebels retired to Cirencester, where they surrendered. They were all put to death, with the exception of Rutland, who had betrayed their plans and deserted to Henry.

This conspiracy sealed Richard's fate, and by the middle of January 1400 he was dead. How did he die? According to the official account, he fell into a state of profound despondency on hearing of the defeat and death of his friends, refused food, and quietly passed away, aged only in his middle thirties. On 29 January his body was conveyed to London, being publicly displayed at various places on the way, and lay for two days in St. Paul's Cathedral, where Henry himself attended a solemn mass, bearing the pall. Afterwards the corpse was taken to King's Langley in Hertfordshire, and delivered to the Black Friars, who buried it in the presence of the Bishop of Lichfield and the abbots of Waltham and St. Albans. The body had displayed no outward marks of violence; yet there is little doubt but that Richard came to a violent end.

According to Shakespeare's play *King Richard II* (Act V), Henry sent St Pierce of Exton to poison the ex-king; but when that failed, he struck him down with his own hand. Richard cried from the floor: 'That hand shall burn in never quenching fire, that staggers thus my person. Exton thy fierce hand hath with the king's blood stained the king's own land. Mount, mount my soul! Thy seat is up on high; whilst my gross flesh sinks downward, here to die.' To which Exton replied: 'As full of valour as of royal blood, Both have I spilt.' As, however, no wounds appeared on the body, this story is manifestly false.

None the less there were plenty of ways in which Richard could have been murdered without showing any external signs: by poison, smothering, or even by the method once employed on Edward II. Most historians believe that he was deliberately starved to death. Despite the public display of the body and the elaborate funeral, rumours, as they had in the case of Edward II, continued to assert that he was still alive, had escaped and was probably hiding in Scotland. The dangerous northern rebellions of 1403-5, led by the Earl of Northumberland, Harry Hotspur and Archbishop Scrope, had as one of their objectives the 'restoration of the true line'; and as late as 1415, when Henry V was about to sail for the invasion of France, a plot, headed by Lord Scrope, was unearthed to overthrow him and reinstate Richard. Yet curiously enough Henry IV's son, Henry V, himself always cherished an affection for Richard, ever since as a youth he had accompanied that king to Ireland,where he was knighted. Then, when Richard fled to north Wales, young Henry went with him, and remained with that doomed monarch, until the latter at Chester persuaded the young man to join his father in London. So when, in 1413, 25-year-old Henry V ascended the throne, he had Richard II's body transferred to Westminster Abbey and buried in a costly tomb.

King Henry VI (1422-1461), that weak, gentle, saintly figure, had inherited from his Valois ancestors a strain of insanity, which from time to time, as in the later case of George III, rendered him incapable of ruling. Inheriting the kingdom, upon the death of his father, Henry V, whilst still in the cradle, he became all his life the puppet of ruthless men; and, after his marriage, he was little more than a docile instument in the hands of his formidable wife, Margaret of Anjou and her favourites. A meek, humble and deeply religious man, he was also a lover of sound learning and the arts; and has left behind him two imperishable memorials of his reign: Eton College near Windsor, and King's College, Cambridge.

Caught up in the Wars of the Roses, which were none of his making, the luckless king, after the defeat of the Lancastrians at the bloody Battle of Towton near Tadcaster in March 1461, was deposed by Yorkist Edward IV. Further fighting followed until the Yorkist victory at Hexham in 1464, and with the now deposed Henry VI being caught in the following year, wandering in disguise in Lancashire with but half a dozen attendants.

The Earl of Warwick led the former Henry VI through the streets of London, his feet bound to the stirrups, to a prison chamber in the Tower. Here he was provided with servants and kindly treated. For as long as Henry's son (an Edward who never reigned), continued to live safely in France, there was no point in putting the older man to death. But in September 1470 the Earl of Warwick, the so-called Kingmaker, changed sides, and together with his son-in-law, George Duke of Clarence, invaded England, causing Edward IV to fly to Burgundy. Henry, once again King Henry VI, emerged from the Tower and was paraded through the streets of London.

Then, in the following March, Edward landed at Ravenspur, to reclaim the throne for the House of York. He entered York in triumph, and, with a rapidly growing army, marched south, by-passing Warwick at Coventry, to advance on London. Archbishop George Neville of York, who had been left in charge of the capital, once again mounted the wretched Henry on a horse and led him through the streets in a vain attempt to whip up the enthusiasm of the citizens for the Lancastrian cause. But the Mayor and Corporation decided that they would not oppose Edward, who had now reached St. Albans; the gates of London flew open, and Henry quickly found himself back in the Tower. For the moment his life was spared; but after the Battles of Barnet and Tewkesbury, where both Warwick and the young Lancastrian prince, Edward, were killed, the reason for this immunity no longer existed.

On Tuesday, 21 May 1471, Edward IV returned in triumph to London; and that same evening the king held a council of war, at which it was decided to eliminate the last of the Lancastrian line in the person of Henry VI. Richard, Duke of Gloucester, was sent with a delegation of noblemen to order the Constable of the Tower, Lord Dudley, to extinguish the feeble candle of Henry's fifty-year lifespan. According to Shakespeare, Gloucester himself stabbed the ex-king to death. This is certainly not true; and it appears he was actually struck down from behind by anonymous murderers as he knelt in prayer at his evening devotions. The next night his body, surrounded by torches and a guard of honour, was borne to St. Paul's, where it lay on a bier, but with only the face uncovered. The unhappy monarch was then buried in the Lady Chapel of Chertsey Abbey. However, this was not to be his last resting place. Rumours spread that miracles were being wrought at his tomb, so Richard III had his remains moved to Windsor. Later, in the reign of Henry VII, Chertsey Abbey claimed them back; this was refused on the grounds that not only had the abbot agreed to their transfer, but had actually assisted at their exhumation with his own hands. However, the request of Westminster Abbey (the traditional burial place of kings) for the body appeared more likely to succeed; especially as it was known that Henry himself in his life-time had had his burial place marked out by the mason (John Thirske), between the tombs of the Confessor and Henry III.

Judgment was actually given in favour of Westminster on 5 March 1498, when the abbey agreed to pay the king £500 to cover the cost of the papal licence and the expense of moving the corpse. It was dependant, however, on Henry's canonisation, for which the Pope was demanding an exorbitant price, and which the mean-minded Henry VII was reluctant to pay. The latter decided therefore to postpone the transfer and the canonisation until his new chapel at Westminster had been completed to house the body. Before that came to pass Henry VII was dead, and his successor Henry VIII never showed any interest either in the canonisation or the translation of his great uncle. In fact Henry VI still reposes in Windsor Chapel, uncanonised.

King Edward V (1483): the thirteen year old boy who was never crowned, none-the-less automatically succeeded to the throne on the death of his father, Edward IV, in April 1483. Preparations had been made for his coronation; but on his way to London from Ludlow Castle, escorted by his uncle, Lord Rivers, and Sir Thomas Vaughan, he was intercepted at Northampton by another uncle, Richard of Gloucester (soon to be Richard III), who had been named in Edward IV's Will as Protector, together with the Duke of Buckingham. Rivers and Vaughan were arrested and subsequently executed; whilst Gloucester brought the young boy to London and lodged him at the Tower in the royal appartments. At first preparations for the coronation continued; and he was joined by his younger brother, Richard, whom their mother, the dowager Queen Elizabeth (having fled to Westminster Abbey for sanctuary) was persuaded to release from her care.

Then, suddenly, it was announced that both princes were illegitimate, since Edward IV had been solemnly betrothed to Eleanor Butler, which in medieval eyes was as good as a marriage. She had been incarcerated in a nunnery, but was still alive at the time of Edward's wedding to Elizabeth Grey. This had been a closely guarded secret, until Bishop Stillington of Bath and Wells, one of the few people in the know, revealed it to Richard of Gloucester. The latter now claimed the throne for himself as the next legitimate heir.

A conspiracy on behalf of Edward V, led by Lord Hastings, a favourite of the late king, was nipped in the bud; Hastings was executed; and the illegitimacy of the princes was ratified by parliament. Gloucester and his wife, Anne Neville, were crowned at Westminster Abbey on 6 July 1483 as Richard III and Queen Anne. Meanwhile the two princes in the Tower were seen for a while playing in the grounds and practising archery; later still their faces were noticed at the window of their appartment; then they disappeared from sight. An Italian visitor to this country, Dominic Mancini, who left England in July 1483 noted these facts in his diary, written in December 1483, along with a suspicion that the princes were now dead, adding however, 'by what manner of death, so far I have not at all discovered'. After the rebellion and execution of the Duke of Buckingham in the autumn of 1483, rumours began to spread that the princes were dead; and these were never denied by Richard.

According to *The History of King Richard III*, written by Sir Thomas More about 1515, Richard had the boys smothered and their bodies buried under a heap of stones at the foot of the staircase leading to their room; and this account was echoed by the historians, Edward Hall and Polydore Vergil. It is, of course, the story upon which Shakespeare based his famous play. But actually Henry VII never accused Richard directly of murdering the princes. He went no further than to say that he had 'shed infants' blood'. Once the Tudors had gone doubts very soon began to be cast upon this theory, especially by Sir George Buc in his five volume *History of the Life and Reign of Richard III*. That was followed in 1768 by Horace Walpole's *Historic Doubts*; and the exoneration of Richard became even more vociferous in the 19th century, culminating in Sir Clement R. Markham's *Richard III : A Doubtful Verdict Reviewed*, in which he fairly and squarely saddled Henry VII himself with the murder. The princes, he argued, were no danger to Richard, since parliament had declared them illegitimate; but Henry Tudor needed Edward IV's children legitimised in order to marry Elizabeth of York (daughter of Edward IV) and so unite warring factions of the red and white roses. Consequently, if the princes had been still alive in the Tower after Richard III's death in the Battle of Bosworth in 1485, they would have represented a serious rivalry for the crown. This version of events was used by Josephine Tey in her famous novel *The Daughter of Time*.

In 1674 workmen, excavating in the area where, according to Sir Thomas More, the princes had been buried under a great heap of stones, unearthed some human bones. These at first were thrown away as rubbish, but later, on the command of Charles II, as many as could be found were retrieved, placed in an urn designed by Sir Christopher Wren and installed in Westminster Abbey. In July 1933 this urn was opened and the bones, part human and part animal, were carefully examined by eminent surgeons and dentists. Their conclusions were as follows: they were the bones of two children, approximately of the ages of the princes in August 1483; but it was impossible to determine the sex of either child, and the stain on the jaw of the elder could not necessarily be attributed to suffocation. So 'The Princes in the Tower', like that of 'The Man in the Iron Mask', still remains one of the great mysteries of history.

Did Richard commit these murders? One of the great arguments in favour of his innocence, is the fact that their mother emerged from her sanctuary and attended Richard's court, along with her daughters. If Elizabeth had really believed that he had murdered her sons, surely such conduct would have been inconceivable. Then, if not Richard, who committed the act? Some recent historians, notably Paul Kendall in his authoritative work: *Richard III*, attribute their deaths either to Henry Stafford, Duke of Buckingham; or John Howard, Duke of Norfolk, both of whom had access to the Tower at the relevant time. Buckingham, as a descendant of Edward III, had his own claim to the throne; and Howard's acquisition of the Dukedom of Norfolk was jeopardised by the fact that the younger of the princes, Richard, had already been given that title. It was therefore in the interests of both these men that the princes should be disposed of, without prior knowledge of the king.

On the other hand the pro-Richard 'Society of the White Boar' maintains that the boys were never murdered at all. There is documentary evidence to show that Richard III's son, Edward, who lived at Sheriff Hutton Castle near York, had high-ranking companions of his own age staying with him, prior to his untimely demise in April 1484. These children, the Society declares, were the two princes, who had been moved there from the Tower. But, when in the summer of 1485 Henry Tudor threatened invasion, they were smuggled out of the country to Flanders, to be cared for by Richard's sister, Margaret, the dowager Duchess of Burgundy.

It has generally been agreed that Edward V was a sickly child, suffering from some infection of the jaw; so the theory goes that he died, from natural causes, either before or after reaching Flanders. However, the younger brother, Richard, re-emerged into the pages of history as Perkin Warbeck, who, indeed, was recognised as Edward IV's son not only by his aunt, but also by the King of Scotland. He gave Henry VII much trouble, but was eventually captured and executed along with his so-called cousin, Edward, Earl of Warwick. Unless therefore hitherto unknown documentary evidence sheds further light on this historical 'Who Done It', the verdict must necessarily remain 'unproven'.

King Charles I (1625-1649) surrendered to the Scots at Newark a year after the Battle of Naseby, hoping thereby to deepen the already wide divisions between them and the English Parliament. He expected to be treated as a guest; but instead was kept prisoner at Newcastle upon Tyne, where he was pressed to accept the Covenant and Presbyterianism. Charles, as always, sought to prevaricate; and so the Scots decided to come to terms with Parliament. Partly in return for handing over the king to a parliamentary commission, the Scots were to receive an instalment of half the sum owed to them for their war services. Charles was lodged at Holmby House, where he was treated with all honour, and negotiations began with Parliament. However, the New Model Army now intervened. It had already refused to go to Ireland or disband until all arrears of pay had been met; and, since it still respected the royal authority, the generals determined to seize Charles' person and negotiate a settlement with him themselves.

So Cromwell ordered Cornet Joyce to carry out this mission; and, upon the king asking for his commission, he merely pointed to his regiment. 'It is one', replied Charles, 'I can read without spelling!' He was taken to Hampton Court, where, walking up and down its gardens, he sought to hammer out a compromise solution with Cromwell, Ireton, and Fairfax. This could well have been reached, if either side had really wanted to do so. But Charles was hoping for a royalist rising, with the Scots this time on his side; and the generals could not carry the soldiers with them in such a deal. For the more extreme puritan troops, backed by their junior officers, wanted Charles brought to trial as The Man of Blood. So fearing 'this brew of hot gospel and cold steel', Cromwell and Ireton decided to suspend negotiations.

Charles now feared for his life. Kingship had notoriously been tempered by successful murder in the past; so, escaping one night from Hampton Court, he made his way to Carrisbrooke Castle in the Isle of Wight. From here he signed a secret agreement with the Scots, whereby royalism and presbyterianism were to be allied against the Independents and the English Army. But Cromwell and Ireton were able to restore discipline in the New Model Army just in time, at the expense of shooting only one agitator.

The Second Civil War of 1648 was soon over. Cromwell crushed the Welsh, and then marched north to defeat the Scots at Preston. Fairfax, for his part, stormed Colchester, where he had its two commanders, Leslie and Lucas, shot. The Cornish rising in the west was also quickly suppressed. Cromwell was furious: describing the war as 'a more prodigious treason than any that had been perfected before; because the former quarrel was that English men should rule over one another; this to vassalise us to a foreign power'. He was now to all intents and purposes a dictator, and the king was finished. None the less the latter refused to fly, as urged by his friends, being already deep in new negotiations with Parliament, and still confident that as king his position was indispensable. He quickly found out his mistake.

Charles was seized by the Army and lodged at Hurst Castle as a prisoner, with scarcely an attendant, being shut into the candleless gloom of a small tower room. He was now convinced that he was going to be murdered; and, whilst being taken south under guard, actually asked his jailer, Colonel Harrison, that question. Harrison replied: 'The Law is equally bound to great and small alike'. But Charles was not afraid of the Law, for a king can do no wrong. He was now housed at Windsor Castle, and all his privileges were restored, whilst a last attempt by the Council of Officers was made to come to terms with him. This the king, in his new found confidence, firmly rebuffed.

Early in January 1649 Pride's Purge reduced the House of Commons to an acquiescent 'Rump' which agreed to the king's trial for treason, 'by levying war against Parliament and the Kingdom of England'. It set up a 'High Court of Justice' consisting of some 135 Commissioners; but no judge would agree to take part, and Fairfax refused to have anything to do with these proceedings. In the end, since no English jurist could be found to frame the indictment, it was undertaken by a Dutchman, Isaac Dorislaus, who cited precedents from the Roman Empire.

On 11 January 1649 Charles was moved to St. James' Palace; and the very next day the trial commenced in Westminster Hall. The king refused at first to plead, laughed to scorn the charge of treason and demanded to know by what authority he was being tried. Bradshaw, the president of the court, replied that he was arraigned before the people of England, who had elected him, to which he received the answer: 'this kingdom has been hereditary for a thousand years', carefully ignoring the election by parliament of Henry IV, and the more than doubtful claims of Henry VII.

Posing now as the champion of the liberties of England, Charles declared: 'If power without laws can make laws, I do not know what subject he is in England that can be sure of his life or anything he calls his own'. The civilians present in the Hall appeared to favour him, and there was a murmur of 'God save the King', which were however drowned by the shouts of the soldiers, 'Justice, Justice'. A request to be heard by the Lords was refused, and the king was given no opportunity to defend himself. Instead by a majority of 68 votes to 67 he was condemned to death as 'The Man of Blood'. For as Winston Church once said: 'One is enough'. On being removed from the Hall Charles exclaimed: 'I am not suffered to speak. Expect what justice other people will have'.

Throughout the trial, which ended on 27 January 1649, the king behaved with the greatest dignity and courage, which much impressed all the beholders. 'Nothing commonplace or mean upon that memorable scene'. Two days later he said farewell to his two younger children, Elizabeth and Henry, Duke of Gloucester (the other members of his family having escaped to the continent); and upon the morning of 30 January, Charles walked from St. James' Palace to Whitehall, where a scaffold had been erected outside Inigo Jones' elegantly proportioned Banqueting House. He wore two shirts as it was a cold day, explaining that otherwise, should he tremble from the cold, the people might think it was from fear.

Only 48 years old, he walked briskly, saying to his guards: 'Step out now'. For some hours the king remained in the Banqueting Hall conversing with his friends and attendants; whilst outside his enemies had become divided. Some of the signatories to the death warrant began to have second thoughts, and Fairfax was furious, reminding his colleagues that to execute Charles merely left them with his eldest son, who was safely abroad. Cromwell, Ireton and Harrison, however, stood firm; and at one o'clock the hour had come for the execution.

The king stepped through a window onto the scaffold attended by Bishop Juxon and other friends. Soldiers, massed in rank after rank, held back the crowds; and although Charles was allowed to speak he found he could only really be heard by those actually with him on the scaffold. He said that he died a good christian and forgave all the world, especially those men who had condemned him to death; to which he added: that had he given way to arbitrary government, and had all the laws changed according to the sword, he need not have suffered, and was a martyr to his people. To his friends he gave some small tokens such as a glove or a ring, and uttered the memorable word 'Remember' to Bishop Juxon. Then, after assisting the executioner to arrange his hair under a small white satin cap, he laid down upon the block.

At his own signal his head was struck off with a single blow, and held up for the people to see. The cry arose: 'This is the head of a traitor'; but it was drowned in the groan of the multitude, who then pressed forward to dip their kerchiefs in the royal blood. 'It was such a groan', wrote a contemporary, 'by the thousands then present as I have never heard before, and desire I may never hear again'. The troops then proceeded to break up the crowds so brutally, that as Philip Henry said: 'I had much ado among the rest to escape home without hurt'. The cult of the martyred king had already begun. Later that day, Cromwell, looking down on the king's body as it lay in its coffin at St. James's Palace, before being taken to Windsor for burial, uttered the words: 'Cruel necessity'. It was said that as Charles' coffin was being carried into St. George's Chapel, Windsor, a fall of snow turned the black velvet pall to white; a sign from Heaven, declared his friends, that he was innocent.

At the Restoration in 1660, of the sixty men who had signed the king's death warrant, a third were dead, a third had fled the country, and only twenty remained. Charles II fought for clemency, and in the event a mere nine were executed, including General Harrison and Hugh Peters, Cromwell's chaplain. The corpses of Cromwell, Ireton and Bradshaw were exhumed from the Abbey, drawn through the streets on a hurdle to Tyburn, and there hanged. Their heads were then cut off and spiked on London Bridge, while the bodies were thrown on a dunghill. Cromwell's head was later recovered, and is now in the possession of Sidney Sussex College, Cambridge, his own old college. Cromwell's daughter, Mary Fauconberg, is believed to have brought her father's body to her home at Newburgh Priory, near Coxwold in North Yorkshire, where a never-opened tomb may today be seen by prior arrangement. John Pym and twenty other parliamentarians were also disinterred, and then reburied in a mass grave outside the Abbey.

So we bring the story of our murdered monarchy to a close.

The tumult and the shouting dies;
The captains and the kings depart.

(Recessional by Rudyard Kipling)

II   Monarchs Killed in Battle

APART FROM THESE SEVEN murdered monarchs, there were four other English kings, who, since 1066 have been killed in battle; while a fifth died violently whilst preparing for war. Their deaths, too, are briefly recorded here:

King Harold (1066). As every British school child knows, the Saxon King Harold was killed in 1066 at the Battle of Hastings, on the south coast of England east of Beachy Head, by an arrow fired by the invading bowmen of William, Duke of Normandy. King Harold had just successfully defeated Norse invaders at the Battle of Stamford Bridge on the River Derwent near York, and the returning forced-march south again left him ill-prepared for renewed successful fighting on 'two fronts' in his one and only year as King of England, leading to his death in battle at the age of 44.

William I (1066-1087). William the Conqueror once he had more or less consolidated his position in England, was compelled from 1071 onwards to devote his considerable martial energies to defending his dukedom of Normandy, which was threatened both by the King of France and the Duke of Anjou. He was, indeed, particularly angered by the French king's ribald remarks about William's growing paunch, promising in return 'to set all France ablaze'. In the spring of 1087 he led his men, sacking and burning, through the streets of Mantes, when his horse stumbled on a red-hot ember, throwing him heavily against the pommel of his saddle, rupturing the bladder. Peritonitis set in, and he was carried in great agony to the priory of St. Gervase at Rouen. Here he lingered through the summer months, dying on 9 September at the age of 60.

24

During his illness he was visited by his two younger sons, William Rufus (to be William II) and Henry (later to be Henry I), naming the former as his successor. 'Authority forsakes a dying king', and after death his attendants stripped the body and plundered the chamber where he lay. The clergy bore him to St. Stephen's Church, Caen, which he had founded; but the funeral was scarcely an edifying one. A citizen of Caen named Ascelan barred the way of the procession in the graveyard, angrily crying out that his father had been deprived of this plot of ground by the late king and demanding justice; he was pacified with an immediate cash payment of sixty shillings.

Richard I (1189-1199). In March 1199 Richard Coeur de Lion, who had claimed but been refused a treasure discovered by one of his vassals near the Castle of Chalus at Limousin in France, was besieging that town, when, reckless as ever, riding too near the castle walls, he was shot in the shoulder near the neck by a cross-bow bolt from the battlements. The wound went deep and was further aggravated by the incompetent manner in which his physician, Marchadeus, extracted the missile.

Gangrene set in and Richard knew that he was dying. He sent for his mother, Queen Eleanor, who was staying nearby, and she nursed him devotedly until the end. With typical courage and calmness Richard set his affairs in order, naming his brother John as the next king. The castle had been taken, and the archer, who had made the fatal shot, captured. Richard ordered the man to be brought before him, pardoned the deed, and even made the prisoner a gift of money. King Richard died on 6 April, at the age of 42, and his body was buried near his father, Henry II, at Fontevraud; but his heart, as was then customary, was extracted from the corpse and interred at Rouen. Immediately after his death, the unfortunate archer was, however, flayed alive by Richard's angry captains.

Richard III (1483-1485). At Bosworth Field, to the west of Leicester, King Richard III (younger brother of Edward IV) appeared to have an army twice the size of that commanded by Henry Tudor (shortly to be Henry VII); but in fact much of it was either disaffected or openly hostile. Indeed, the only contingent that actually fought for Richard was led by the Duke of Norfolk and his son, Lord Surrey. When the former was slain and the latter captured it became obvious that the battle was lost. Lord Stanley refused to obey orders; and upon Richard threatening to execute his eldest son Lord Strange (whom he held hostage), Stanley calmly replied that he had other sons, and moved menacingly nearer the conflict, with the apparent intention of joining the enemy. None the less Lord Strange was not executed. Again, upon the king telling the Earl of Northumberland to support Norfolk, he declined to move.

It has been said that Richard III scorned to fly; but, surrounded as he was by hostile forces and inaccessible marshlands, his best chance of escape lay in the action he took, namely, surrounded by the faithful members of his household, to charge down on what appeared to be the weakest link in the enemy lines, and make a break through. No doubt the primary aim was to kill Henry Tudor; for once the Pretender was dead, his army was likely to break and run. But, even failing this, Richard himself might very well get away to fight another day.

It was, of course, a tremendous gamble, since they would be riding across the front of the six thousand red-coated horsemen under the command of Sir William Stanley, who, like Northumberland, had been standing idly by, uncommitted, awaiting the issue of the battle. The gamble never came off. 35-year-old Richard almost hacked his way through to Henry. Indeed some writers have alleged that he actually crossed swords with him, but as the king was wielding a battle-axe this appears extremely unlikely. At this juncture however, Stanley and his men made up their minds and charged down upon him. The little troop of scarcely a hundred men was overwhelmed, and Richard himself died from multiple blows.

In Shakespeare's famous words, 'A horse, a horse, my kingdom for a horse', shouted Richard of York. The golden crown he wore on his helmet flew off into a neighbouring thorn bush, from which it was later retrieved by Stanley and handed to Henry Tudor. The king's body was stripped of its armour, and the naked bloody corpse, flung over a pack horse, and taken to Leicester, where, after being exposed to the public view, it was buried in Grey Friars Abbey.

Eventually Henry VII provided a stone covering for the grave, which, alas, was desecrated at the Reformation, and Richard's bones were cast into the River Soar. The Richard III Society has recently placed a monument to the king in Leicester Cathedral; and there is also an inscription near the bridge over the River Soar. Whatever his faults Richard undoubtedly possessed the virtue of courage: 'to die like men, and fall like one of the princes'. *(A visit to the Bosworth Field Heritage Centre is recommended.)*

William III (**1688-1702**), that cold, serious, unpopular, foreign monarch, was preparing the Grand Alliance of Holland, Austria and England against Louis XIV of France, when, during the morning of 20 February 1702, he went riding in the park round Hampton Court on his favourite horse, Sorrel. Sorrel stumbled into a fresh mole-hill, throwing the king heavily and breaking his collar-bone. This was set and all might have been well, except that William insisted on being taken immediately by coach to Kensington Palace. This bumpy journey not only aggravated the injury, but added to the shock that he had already suffered to his normally frail physique. He contracted a fever and died on 8 March. For years afterwards jubilant Jacobites drank a toast: 'to the little gentleman in black velvet' in memory of the mole-hill which caused this accident.

Calm and cool as always William III went on transacting business until the end, and with far-sighted wisdom, in his last hours, commended Marlborough to his successor, Queen Anne, as the fittest man to guide her councils and command her armies. William was buried at Westminster Abbey in a new vault below the southern aisle, of Henry VII's Chapel, where he lies with Charles II, together with William's wife Mary, and her sister Anne (both daughters of James II), alongside Anne's numerous but tragically short-lived children. Among the tourist attractions at Westminster Abbey are wax effigies, which include the figures of William and Mary.

The last British sovereign to lead his army into battle was **George II (1727-1760)**, who defeated the French at the village of Dettingen near Aschaffenburg in Germany in 1743.

\